Scrambled egg

WENDY BINKS

STRIPEY THE EMU CHICK lived at Fair Dinkum Flats with his twenty-nine brothers and sisters and their parents, Crikey and Sheila.

Stripey and his sister Leggy often went off running together. Everyone knows that emus are the fastest runners in all of Australia, and both chicks were determined to run as fast as Crikey and Sheila when they grew up.

One day the two chicks were running at Belly Button Bluff when suddenly they heard a loud squawking and screeching. It came from the old ghost gum where Fluster the corella had her nesting hole. Fluster was jumping up and down and flapping her wings. She was very upset.

"What's wrong?" asked Stripey.

"My egg! My egg!" she shrieked, pointing at a small white egg lying at the base of the gumtree.

"It must have fallen out!" screeched Fluster. "It needs to stay warm for my chick to hatch. What can I do? What can I do?"

Stripey and Leggy thought very hard.

"I know!" Leggy said. "We could ask Bluey the red kangaroo to put the egg in her warm pouch until we can get it back into the nest."

Fluster flapped her wings. "That's a great idea! But hurry, please hurry!"

Stripey and Leggy ran as fast as they could to Dusty Bucket Gully, where Bluey lived with her joey, Socks. The big red kangaroo looked up as they skidded to a stop beside her. "Hey, what's the hurry, you two?" she asked.

"Please," Stripey panted, "could you come to Belly Button Bluff? One of Fluster's eggs has fallen onto the ground. We hoped you might put it in your pouch while we work out how to get it back in her nest."

Bluey smiled. "Sure, I'd be happy to help. Come on, let's go!" Socks jumped head-first into her pouch and they all set off.

Back at Belly Button Bluff, Fluster squawked with relief when she saw the chicks with Bluey. Socks climbed out of the warm pouch and Bluey carefully picked up the egg and placed it inside. They all looked up at the nest-hole which was far too high in the gum tree for anyone to reach. Socks hoped the problem would be solved before night time because he wanted his soft, cosy bed back.

Just then Bluey's eyes widened. "Uh-oh! I felt the egg move. Maybe it's hatching!"

"It can't be. It's too early! Too early!" Fluster shrieked.

Bluey pulled open her pouch and everyone peered inside. Sure enough, the small white egg was jiggling and wiggling and there was a tiny hole in the shell. Bluey reached in, took it out and placed it gently on the ground in front of them.

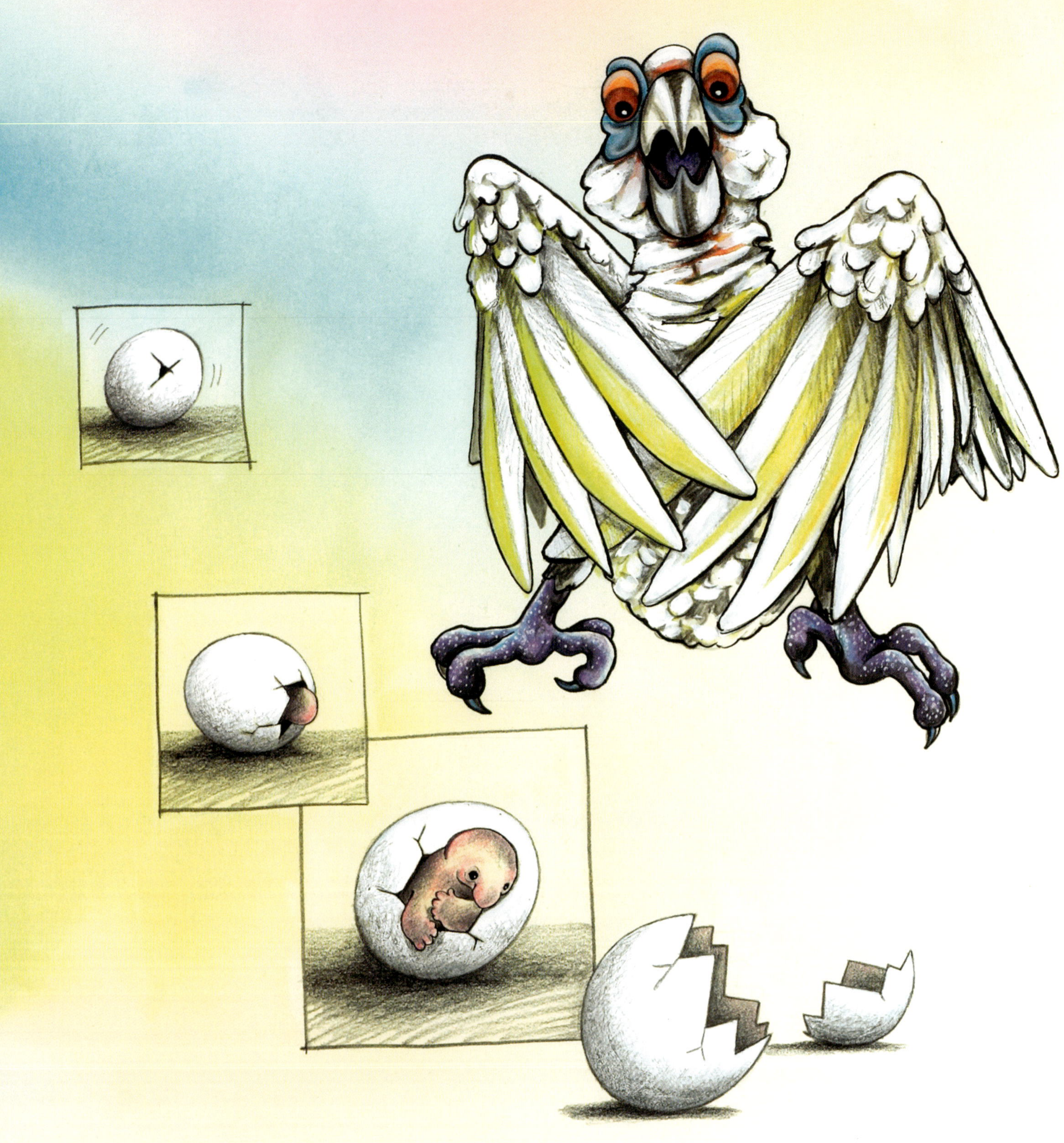

Fluster clapped her wings in anticipation. There was more jiggling and wiggling, the hole grew larger and … a *nose* appeared.

A nose?

Fluster was so amazed that she couldn't squawk or screech or shriek. The egg opened some more and out tumbled the strangest creature any of them had ever seen.

It was definitely NOT a corella chick. Not a chick of any kind, in fact. They all looked at Fluster, who giggled. "Oops, I guess it didn't fall from my nest after all. I was never much good at counting. Someone else must have lost it here."

"But what *is* it?" Socks asked his mother.

"I don't know," Bluey replied. "It looks just like … a grub."

"What shall we do with it?" asked Leggy.

"We need to find its mother," Stripey declared.

"But we don't know who she is," Leggy said, "except that she is not a bird."

"Good luck!" squawked Fluster, and flew up to her nest to keep her own eggs warm.

Bluey very carefully picked up the squirming grub and popped it back in her pouch.

"What other animals lay eggs?" she wondered.

"I know!" said Leggy. "How about Snap the swamp turtle? She lays eggs. It's not too far to Broken Springs."

Snap was dozing in the shallows at Broken Springs when they arrived.

"Hi, Snap," Bluey greeted her. "Can you help us? We're looking for the mother of this baby." And she stretched her pouch open so that Snap could see the tiny hairless creature.

"Goodness! Well, it certainly isn't a turtle baby," said Snap. "What is it?"

"We don't know," Stripey told her. "It hatched from an egg but it isn't a bird and now we know it isn't a turtle. Have you any idea who its mother could be?"

"Hmm. What about Flatfoot the platypus?" suggested Snap. "She lays eggs. She lives just upstream at Two-Bob Bank."

So off they went to look for Flatfoot the platypus.

At Two-Bob Bank, Flatfoot was hiding in the reeds. Platypuses are never very fond of visitors. "Excuse us for disturbing you, Flatfoot," said Leggy politely, "but we hope you can help us. We're looking for the mother of this baby." Flatfoot came out of the reeds and Bluey showed her the grub.

"Goodness! Well, it certainly isn't a platypus baby," Flatfoot said. "What is it?"

"We don't know," Leggy said, "it hatched from an egg, but it isn't a bird, it isn't a turtle, and now we know it isn't a platypus. Have you any idea who its mother could be?"

"Hmm. What about Strewth the frilled-neck lizard? She lays eggs. She lives beyond the Black Stump in Vegemite Valley."

Bluey thanked Flatfoot, and they left to find Strewth.

At Vegemite Valley they found Strewth sunbaking on top of the Black Stump.

"Hi, Strewth," said Bluey. "Can you help us? We're looking for the mother of this baby." She held open her pouch and Strewth peered in.

"Goodness! Well, it certainly isn't a lizard baby," Strewth declared. "What is it?"

"We don't know," Socks said boldly. "It hatched from an egg but it isn't a bird, it isn't a turtle, it isn't a platypus, and now we know it isn't a lizard. Have you any idea who its mother could be?"

"Hmm," Strewth replied. "How about Shuffle the echidna? She lays eggs. She lives on Don't-Stand-Still Hill."

What a funny name for a hill, Socks thought, as they set off again.

Shuffle was eating lunch when they found her.

"Hi, Shuffle," said Bluey, "Can you help us? We're looking for the mother of this baby." And she showed Shuffle the tiny grub in her pouch.

"Goodness gracious! That's a puggle!"

"A *puggle*?" Socks repeated. "What on earth is that?"

"A baby echidna, of course," Shuffle told him. And she patted her tummy…

…then she felt it again and looked down in horror. Her pouch was empty! "Oh, my precious egg!" she cried. "It's disappeared!" She thought for a moment, and then looked up at Bluey. "Where did you find this puggle?"

"It hatched from an egg we found at Belly Button Bluff," said the kangaroo.

"That's where I was this morning!" Shuffle exclaimed. "The egg must have fallen out of my pouch! Oh, thank you for bringing my puggle back to me!"

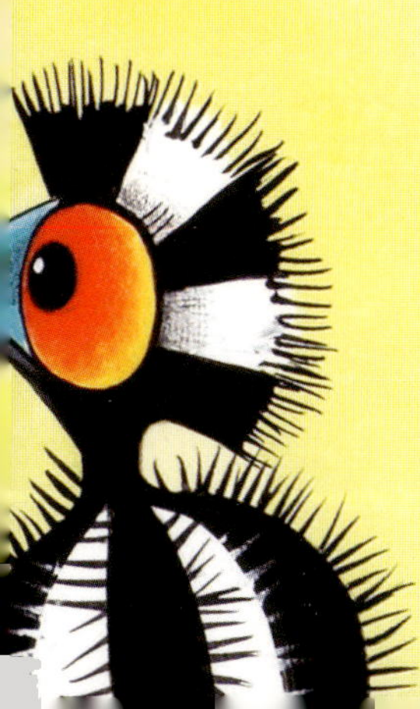

Bluey gently lifted out the tiny wriggling puggle and laid it on the ground. Shuffle nuzzled her baby tenderly then nudged it into her own little pouch.

Bluey, Socks, Stripey and Leggy all smiled.

The next moment, however, their smiles vanished. They had been standing still on Don't-Stand-Still Hill far too long and ANTS were now scurrying up their legs.

"Let's get out of here!" Bluey said as she hopped and danced. Socks dived into her pouch and together they bounded away for Dusty Bucket Gully.

As for Stripey and Leggy, they ran all the way back to Fair Dinkum Flats faster than they'd ever run before ... leaving a trail of ants behind them.

INTERESTING FACTS

ABOUT SOME OF THE ANIMALS IN THIS BOOK

EMU: Emus are the second largest bird in the world after the ostrich. They belong to the Ratite family of flightless birds. Other Ratites are kiwis, cassowaries, and rheas. After the female lays her 10-20 large dark-green eggs, she leaves and the eggs are incubated and the chicks reared solely by the male parent. The chicks have stripes when hatched, which help to camouflage them.

RED KANGAROO: The largest species of kangaroo, they inhabit arid northern areas of Australia. The females are often known as "blue flyers". The baby is born the size of a jellybean and crawls up a pathway licked by the mother to reach her pouch. The mother may have 3 babies growing at the same time: one in the pouch attached to a teat, a larger baby outside the pouch drinking a different mixture of milk from one of the other 3 teats, and the third as an embryo in suspended animation in the womb, waiting for a vacancy.

ECHIDNA: This unusual creature has a beak like a bird, a pouch like a marsupial, produces milk like a mammal, lays eggs like a reptile, and may live for up to 50 years. The echidna is one of only 3 monotremes (mammals which lay eggs.) The others are the platypus and the long-beaked echidna of Papua New Guinea. The name "echidna" derives from Ekhidna, a Greek Goddess who was half-reptile and half-mammal. After the single leathery egg is laid it is guided by the echidna's tail into the shallow pouch and then 10 days later the 1.3cm long "puggle" is hatched. The puggle stays in the pouch for about 7 weeks or until it starts to grow spines. The mother then leaves it in her den, visiting it every 5-10 days. Echidnas are found throughout Australia wherever there are ants, which are caught on its long tongue coated with sticky saliva. The echidna is quite intelligent and is a great escape artist.

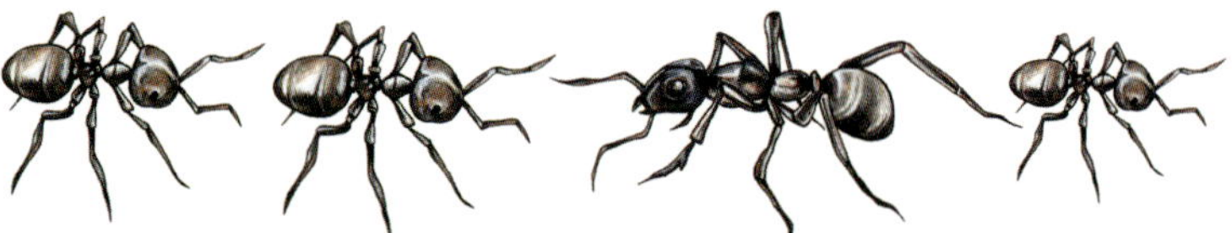

PLATYPUS: "Platypus" is Greek for "Flatfoot". When the first specimen was sent from Australia to England, scientists thought it was an elaborate fake. The platypus spends most of its time in the water where impulses from small crustaceans and other edible water dwellers are picked up by electro sensors on its leathery duck-like bill. The female has no pouch. She lays her 2 or 3 eggs in her den, where they are incubated and suckled. Like the echidna, the platypus secretes milk from its skin pores.

WESTERN SWAMP TURTLE: Australia's most endangered reptile. It occurs in only two swamps near Perth, Western Australia, and may be seen at the Perth Zoo, which has a successful breeding program. These turtles "aestivate" during dry periods, finding holes in the mud and slowing all their body processes as they wait for the first rains. The female lays 1-3 eggs.

FRILL-NECKED LIZARD:
It lives in hot, dry areas, and spends most of its life up a tree. If it is alarmed it opens its mouth wide to activate its neck frill, which makes it look larger and more ferocious. It runs on its hind legs. The female lays 20-25 eggs, and the baby lizards look after themselves when hatched.

For Mum and Dad

Thanks for hatching me.

First published in Australia in 2007 by
Stunned Emu Press, Fremantle Western Australia

Reprinted 2008, 2014, 2019, 2022
info@wendybinks.com.au

National Library of Australia
Cataloguing-in-Publication data:

Binks, Wendy.
Scrambled egg : another Stripey adventure.

For children aged two to eight years.
ISBN 9780646479293 (pbk.).

I. Title.

A823.4

Written and Illustrated by Wendy Binks
Edited by Barbara Ker Wilson
Book Design and Production by Brown Cow Design
Printed by Quality Press
PRODUCED WHOLLY IN AUSTRALIA